"This book is a treasure! In a clear and engaging style, Father Tobin offers the distilled wisdom of his years of pastoral and personal experience on the crucial subject of forgiveness. His profound and practical suggestions are a real gift for this difficult challenge which all of us face on the human journey."

PATRICIA LIVINGSTON, AUTHOR OF *LET IN THE LIGHT: FACING THE HARD STUFF WITH HOPE*

"In writing about forgiveness, Father Eamon Tobin has performed an invaluable service for the Christian community and beyond. His book is insightful, comprehensive, and very reader-friendly. Father tackles the hard questions about forgiveness with honesty and pastoral sensitivity. I especially appreciated his many concrete examples throughout the book and his prayer suggestions."

SISTER MELANNIE SVOBODA, SND, AUTHOR OF *TRAITS OF A HEALTHY SPIRITUALITY*

"Christians know forgiveness is an important part of healthy spirituality so why is it sometimes so hard to forgive? Father Eamon Tobin offers practical, easy-to-follow wisdom in this latest revision of his book. Anyone who has ever struggled with this issue will find an uplifting message of hope in these pages."

BARBARA SHLEMON RYAN, RN, PRESIDENT, BELOVED MINISTRY, AUTHOR OF *HEALING THE HIDDEN SELF* AND *HEALING THE WOUNDS OF DIVORCE*

"To forgive another is very difficult. To distinguish between forgiving and feeling that we have forgiven others is critically important for a person's inner peace. To reconcile with another is complex and not always possible.

"Father Eamon Tobin's helpful booklet tells us why we should and how we can deal with each of those real-life challenges."

FATHER JOSEPH CHAMPLIN, SEMIRETIRED PRIEST AND AUTHOR

"Most books on forgiveness tell you about the need to forgive. This book offers the reader lots of practical suggestions on how to make forgiveness a reality."

FATHER MATT LINN, S.J.

How to Forgive Yourself and Others

Steps to Reconciliation

Newly Revised and Expanded Third Edition

FATHER EAMON TOBIN

Liguori
LIGUORI, MISSOURI

Imprimi Potest:
Thomas D. Picton, C.Ss.R.
Provincial, Denver Province
The Redemptorists

Imprimatur:
Most Reverend Robert J. Hermann
Auxiliary Bishop
Archdiocese of St. Louis

ISBN-10: 0-7648-1532-6
ISBN-13: 978-0-7648-1532-4
Library of Congress Control Number: 2006927162

Scripture quotations are from the *New Revised Standard Version of the Bible,*
© 1989 by the Division of Christian Education of the National Council of the
Churches of Christ in the USA. Used by permission. All rights reserved.

The quote on pages 8–10 was reprinted with permission from *The Healing
Power of Forgiveness,* by Jean Maalouf. Copyright © 2005; all rights reserved. Twenty-Third Publications, New London, CT 06320.

Liguori Publications, a nonprofit corporation, is an apostolate of the Redemptorists. To learn more about the Redemptorists, visit Redemptorists.com.

To order, call 1-800-325-9521
www.liguori.org

Contents

Foreword

Nothing is clearer in the gospel than Jesus' command to forgive life's hurts and injustices. Yet, following this command of Jesus is surely one of life's greatest challenges. Many, if not most people, firmly believe that it is *impossible,* if not foolish or even stupid, to forgive someone who has deeply offended us or done us a grave injustice. Why should anyone forgive such people?

Even if we had a desire to forgive and move beyond life's hurts and injustices, most of us received little or no guidance in this area while growing up. When I was growing up, I learned a model of forgiveness and reconciliation that left much to be desired. If hurt was inflicted by word or deed, rarely did anyone talk about the hurt experienced or express sorrow for it. Rarely did I hear the words "I'm sorry; please forgive me" or "I forgive you." What usually happened was something like this: A hurt occurred through word or deed, the parties involved had a "falling out," then a silent period of a few hours, days, or weeks followed. Then one party waited silently for the other person to make the first move. Finally, either through the grace of God or the tediousness of the silence, one of the parties began to talk again. In a husband-wife situation, it was usually the wife who made the first move. But the reconciliation nearly always occurred without any discussion of the hurt that caused the alienation, and seldom did anyone say, "I'm sorry; please forgive me." I suppose the model was okay in that the relationship was renewed. Still, I wonder what happened to all the hurt that was rarely, if ever, talked about.

This booklet was born out of two personal experiences with forgiveness and reconciliation. While neither experience was a huge hurt, I nevertheless experienced fierce rage, anger, and hateful thoughts and feelings toward the two individuals I had a falling out with. I had absolutely no desire to communicate with them nor to speak of forgiving them. All I wanted to do was punish them in some way.

Yet several weeks later I reconciled with both people. How did this happen? How did I move from a place of rage, anger, hate, and a desire to punish to a place of forgiveness and reconciliation? This booklet will answer this important question. After the healing of the hurt, I spent some time reflecting on how I came, with the grace of God, to forgive and reconcile the hate and alienation I experienced. Then I started to share the steps I went through in homilies. People responded very positively to my homilies and started to ask me for a copy of them.

Then I noticed that many of the people who came to me in confession and to see me at the parish office often had forgiveness issues that they were unable to move through. As a result they got stuck spiritually. It is not easy to have an honest and open relationship with God while we are *deliberately* and *intentionally* holding on to a big grudge and showing absolutely no desire to forgive. This is a bad place to be spiritually and emotionally. The good news is that it doesn't have to be that way if we are willing to cooperate with God's grace and follow the practical steps offered in this book.

This book was written in 1983. It was revised and expanded in 1993. Recently, I felt a need to revise and expand the '93 edition. I have come to realize that forgiveness is indeed a very complex issue. Many people misunderstand what forgiveness is and isn't. Many people are not able to name what may be blocking them from making progress in this area. Also, in working with people and as I struggle to forgive life's hurts, I have stumbled on many new insights and ways to help deal with life's hurts.

If you read one or both of the previous editions of this booklet and found them helpful, I have no doubt that you will find this newly *revised* and *expanded* edition even more helpful. Every section of the previous edition has been revised and expanded and some new sections have been added. If you are presently struggling to forgive a hurt, I feel confident that you will find the insights and prayer suggestions offered here to be helpful.

I am grateful to the publishers at Liguori for allowing me to revise and expand the original booklet a second time. I am most grateful to my dedicated secretary, Maria Sittig, for the many times she typed this manuscript as I worked on it. My prayer is that you the reader will find it helpful.

Fr. Eamon Tobin

FATHER EAMON TOBIN
MARCH 17, 2006, FEAST OF SAINT PATRICK

Introduction

Some years ago I listened to a man give a talk about forgiveness. The man had come to lose all respect for his father. But he also felt that there was something missing in his spiritual life despite the fact that he came to church regularly and tried to live a good life. Then one day, moved by the Holy Spirit, the man picked up the phone and said, "Dad, I need to ask for your forgiveness for all the resentment I have been harboring toward you." Even though the father was not very receptive, it did not matter as far as the *spiritual life* of the caller was concerned. He had done what he needed to do. Immediately, he felt a new closeness to God and a new joy entered his life. Also, his prayers of petition for victory over some personal weaknesses started to be answered. This simple story is a great example of the *power* of forgiveness. Through his willingness to ask his father's forgiveness and to forgive him for any hurt he did to him, this man was freed from the burden of resentment. Joy was restored to his life and his renewed relationship with God bore fruit as he sought God's help with his own personal struggles.

When I listen to some very painful hurts and injustices that some people have had to endure, I do understand why they would have absolutely no desire to forgive and let go of hurts and wrongs done to them. I even understand why some people may conclude that it would be wrong to forgive some hurts and grave injustices. Some people find it repulsive to even think about forgiving certain hurts. Unfortunately, the consequence of such a stance is that people are trapped in a sea of bitterness and continue to be controlled emotionally by those who have inflicted a terrible hurt or injustice upon them. When we choose not to forgive, we knowingly or unknowingly choose to cheat ourselves of the joy of living. When we live life with resentment in our hearts, our resentment becomes the lens through which we see reality and people. We see them not as they are but how our resentment wants us to see.

Others who have been grievously hurt feel that forgiveness is way beyond their reach. On a *human* level, forgiveness is beyond many people's reach. That is why we often hear the saying "to err is human, but to forgive is divine." Yet, with the grace of God *all* things are possible—even forgiving what seems like an unforgivable sin or crime.

Inspiring Examples of Forgiveness

One thing that should help us to believe that forgiveness *is* always possible is listening to stories about *ordinary* people who decided to forgive what seemed like unforgivable sins, crimes, and hurts. The following are six inspiring examples of people who made a decision to forgive what could easily be called an unforgivable wrong or crime:

During the riots in the aftermath of the Rodney King trial in Los Angeles, California, a truck driver named Reggie Denny was pulled from his truck and severely beaten. When the case came to trial, Denny stunned the courtroom when he offered to forgive those who almost killed him. Later Denny said that only by forgiving the perpetrators could he put the painful event behind him and move on with his life.

When the Truth and Reconciliation Commission was set up in South Africa to heal the hurts of decades of apartheid and human abuses, an American couple, Peter and Linda Biehl, went to South Africa to meet and embrace the people who killed their twenty-six-year-old daughter.

After spending twenty-seven years in jail for plotting against South Africa's apartheid government, Nelson Mandela said: "As I walked out the door toward the gate that would lead to my freedom, I knew if I didn't leave my bitterness and hatred behind, I'd still be in prison."

In June 2005, Ivon Harris and his daughter Sarah were both killed when they walked in on a robbery of their home. Nancy Harris, Ivon's wife and Sarah's mother, publicly forgave their killer, Russell Sedelmaier. In court Nancy said: "Because I value the gift of life and I know God forgives and loves all of us, especially you Russell, I forgive you and I support a sentence of natural life."

Father Jenco, one of the Beirut hostages, forgave those who had starved, degraded, and brutalized him. He said that only when he was able to forgive his kidnappers was he able to enjoy his freedom.

Shortly after the tragic shootings at Columbine High School in Littleton, Colorado, at least two parents publicly said that they had forgiven the killers of their children.

Fortunately for the vast majority of us, we never have to forgive wrongs or crimes like the above. Most of the issues we deal with are relational hurts between family members, friends, neighbors, fellow parishioners, or co-workers. I realize that some such hurts can be very big, but many are not, and yet we choose to hold on to grudges about some hurts for years. Sadly, many people take their hurts to their grave.

Chapter One

Defining Forgiveness: What It Is and Isn't

Having a clear sense of what forgiveness is and isn't can be a big help as we face this difficult task. Let's first name some of the things that forgiveness is *not*.

What Forgiveness Isn't

- Forgiveness does not necessarily mean that we must forget a hurt or injustice. We often hear the advice "forgive and forget." Sometimes it is not possible to forget some hurts and sometimes it is not even wise to do so. Some hurts and injustices are too big and painful to remove totally from our memory. What we can and should seek to do is to let go of the resentments connected with the hurt. If we don't, these resentments will continue to wound us, cloud the way we see reality, and control our actions. Also, while we may sometimes be able to totally forget some hurts, it is not necessarily wise to forget *all* hurts. We may need to remember some hurts to help us to not allow them to happen again. For example, if we do not remember how a person abused us, we run the risk of allowing such behavior to occur again. Also, remembering hurts that are forgiven and healed will enable us to offer understanding, compassion, and help to others in need of healing.

- Forgiveness doesn't mean that we surrender our right to justice. For example, if we know someone has cheated us of a lot of money, forgiveness doesn't mean that we surrender our right to seek justice. The late Pope John Paul II forgave Ali Agca, the man who tried to kill him, but he didn't request that he be released from jail. Neither did Nancy Harris ask that the killer of her husband and daughter be released. Forgiving someone who breaks our trust doesn't mean that we give him back his job. I sometimes say to people, we shouldn't confuse forgiveness with stupidity. Jesus did indeed ask us to forgive, but he didn't ask us to be stupid in our dealings with others.

- Forgiveness does not necessarily mean that I have to relate to or befriend my offender. This is especially true if my offender shows no sorrow or remorse for the wrong he/she did. Of course, some situations may demand that we try to relate well to our offender, such as when it involves a married couple or friend whom we desire to continue to have a relationship with. It is also very desirable that divorced parents who have children, especially young children get along for the sake of the children. Also, it is desirable that coworkers and parishioners get along for the sake of the community. But the good news is that we can love and forgive someone without befriending them.

- Forgiveness doesn't mean that I have to put up with intolerable behavior. If a spouse or anyone else abuses us, we should do everything in our power to resist such behavior. Forgiveness does not ask that we become doormats for nasty people. Both Mahatma Gandhi and Dr. Martin Luther King, Jr. taught their followers to resist those who did them wrong.

- Forgiveness doesn't mean excusing, condoning, or minimizing the wrong inflicted on us. Jesus never suggested that we do any of the above. He only asks that we forgive.

- Forgiveness doesn't mean that we never have negative feelings toward our offender. As we shall see later there is a difference between the *forgiveness* of a hurt and the *total healing* of a hurt.

- Forgiveness does not mean that we have to like our offender. I doubt Jesus liked the Pharisees, yet I assume he forgave them their offenses against him.

What Forgiveness Is

- Forgiveness is a process (which may take a day, a year, or a lifetime) during which we seek to eliminate from mind and heart all resentment and hurt feelings that we have because of what someone did or said to us.
- Forgiveness is the spiritual surgery that we perform on ourselves (with the help of God's grace) to free ourselves from all the venom we feel as the result of a hurt or injustice.
- Forgiveness is a gift we give ourselves so that we do not remain stuck in the past and in our pain, living as victims of some big hurt or injustice. When we are able to forgive, we move from being the victim of our story to being the hero of it.

Forgiveness is the powerful assertion that bad things will not ruin your today even though they may have spoiled your past.

JEAN MAALOUF

We know that forgiveness is occurring or has occurred when the distance between our offender and us is a peaceful distance and not a hostile one. We know that forgiveness is occurring when we can pray for our offender, wish him or her well and let go of all desire to get even.

Chapter Two

*Three Good Reasons
to Forgive*

**Reason 1: God's word tells us to do so, not once but many
times.**

In Matthew 18:21–22, Peter asks Jesus: "'Lord, if
another member of the church sins against me, how often should I forgive? As many as seven times?' Jesus said
to him, 'Not seven times, but, I tell you, seventy-seven
times.'" Then Jesus goes on to tell a parable about an
official who had been forgiven a huge debt, but who re-
fused to forgive his fellow servant a much lesser debt.
At the end of the parable, Jesus says: "Should you not
have had mercy on your fellow slave, as I had mercy on
you?...So my heavenly Father will also do to every one of
you, if you do not forgive your brother or sister from your
heart" (33, 35).

In Mark 11:25, Jesus says to us: "Whenever you
stand praying, forgive, if you have anything against any-

one; so that your Father in heaven may also forgive you your trespasses." Jesus is saying to us that his love and healing cannot flow into us unless we allow it to flow out to others.

In the book of Sirach 27:30—28:1-4, we hear the following challenging words: "Anger and wrath, these also are abominations, yet a sinner holds on to them. The vengeful will face the Lord's vengeance, for he keeps a strict account of their sins. Forgive your neighbor the wrong he has done, and then your sins will be pardoned when you pray. Does anyone harbor anger against another, and expect healing from the Lord? If one has no mercy toward another like himself, can he then seek pardon for his own sins?"

Lewis Smedes writes: "When we forgive we walk in stride with our forgiving God." One thing that motivated me to seek God's help to forgive was that I felt very hypocritical before God and others while I was *deliberately* carrying a hardened heart toward another. How could I sincerely pray or receive holy Communion when I deliberately held onto grudges and was unwilling to take any steps to heal the hurts.

For many of us, forgiveness, especially of a big hurt or wrong, may be the toughest thing we may ever do emotionally and spiritually. It may stretch us way beyond what we thought we were capable of. For most, if not all of us, forgiveness goes against the grain. It seems unnatural. Jesus' command to forgive may even seem repulsive and outrageous and even stupid.

Yet forgiveness is what God's word clearly asks of us. In the above-cited texts, it is clear that God expects his followers to be generous with mercy just as he is generous with us. In a lifetime, God will have forgiven us thousands of times. Why would we who call ourselves his followers think we shouldn't have to show the same mercy to those who offend us? It is also clear from the above text that an unforgiving heart hurts our relationship with our Lord and hinders his healing from coming into us. People in the healing ministry all agree that deliberately holding onto hurts and wrongs is a big obstacle to people receiving God's healing on a physical, emotional, and spiritual level.

Forgiveness is Jesus' medicine for hurts and wrongs inflicted upon us just as his mercy is the medicine that heals us of the guilt associated with our sins and wrongdoing. When Jesus commands us to forgive we must try hard to trust that he knows what he is doing. Would the Lord prescribe evil or the impossible for us? He prescribes the medicine of forgiveness so that our hearts would be free of the resentment and desire for revenge that steals our peace and joy and wounds us emotionally, spiritually, and even physically. So the first and primary reason to forgive hurts and wrongs is that God's word clearly tells us to do so over and over.

Reason 2: To free our hearts from the destructive power of unforgiveness.

In his excellent book, *The Healing Power of Forgiveness*, Jean Maalouf writes:

> *The benefits of forgiveness have been presented by numerous studies on forgiveness. These studies were conducted in the fields of psychology, medicine, social science, and religion, and they concur in establishing the importance of positive emotions: gratitude, faith, love, forgiveness, hope, caring, and so on. According to these studies, such emotions and virtues have a definite impact on our cardiovascular functioning in particular, and our well-being in general...*
>
> *Indeed, people who practice forgiveness report fewer health problems, feel better psychologically and emotionally, have less stress, and increase the efficient response of their immune system.*
>
> *On the other hand, it has also been proven that bitterness, resentment, and anger can be a fertile soil for malignant growths. I read a story about a woman with breast cancer who visited a spiritual counselor. This woman was suffering for some time because she had undergone several operations while the cancer was spreading throughout her system. The counselor advised her to spend some time alone every day, to medi-*

tate, and to forgive everybody and everything. So she did. Among many different lines she read and meditated on, one particularly drew her attention, when St. Paul recommended to "put on the breastplate of faith and love" (1 Thessalonians 5:8). This line inspired her prayer: Christ is healing me. I put on the breastplate of faith and love and forgiveness and righteousness. I cast all my burdens of injury, hurt, resentment, and bitterness on Christ who is my savior and who sets me free. I am free of every illness. I am healthy. Thank you, God.

For several days, she prayed this way with a heart full of love, hope, and determination. Subsequently, to the astonishment of her doctor, the lump in her breast disappeared and she was completely healed.

This story is one of many similar stories that can be found in the medical records to prove that forgiveness and love have the power to dissolve gallstones, cancers, tumors, and other similar diseases. What the medical records tell us is that, when we are in a state of unforgiveness, our bodies start to manufacture extra chemicals—like adrenaline, adrenocorticotrophic hormone, and cortisone—that build up in the bloodstream. If a situation like this continues for a while unchecked, gastric ulcers and other serious illnesses can result.

Bitter thoughts make bitter cells. Better thoughts make better cells. Forgiving and loving thoughts create healing cells (pp.35–37).

To choose not to enter into the forgiveness process is to choose to give our offender ongoing control over our emotional, spiritual, and physical life. Does that seem smart? I don't think so. Yet, that is exactly what we are doing when we choose not to enter into the difficult process of forgiveness. Just think about it, our offender may have moved forward with his/her life, but he/she continues to control us and keep us miserable. Refusing to enter into the forgiveness process is a choice to inflict a continuous wound on ourselves. It is like refusing to deal with a cancerous wound in our bodies. In his book *10 Secrets for Success and Inner Peace*, Wayne Dyer writes: "Resentment is like venom that continues to pour through your system, doing it poisonous damage long after being bitten by a snake. It's not the bite that kills you; it's the venom." Thousands of years ago, Confucius said: "Those who cannot forgive others break the bridge over which they themselves must pass."

Reason 3: When we forgive, we make our world less violent and more loving.

The media reminds us daily of the hate and animosity that exists in our world. We may even find ourselves saying: Why does it have to be like this? Why can't people settle their differences peacefully? And yet, we ourselves may be guilty of perpetuating hate and animosity in our little piece of the world.

In fact, we are guilty of doing just that as long as we deliberately choose to hold onto grudges and resentments. We are adding more darkness to an already dark world. We may be active participants in keeping a negative atmosphere alive and well in our home, workplace, and church. But when we choose to enter into the forgiveness process we are choosing to overcome the darkness of unforgiveness with love. We become peacemakers whom Jesus called true children of God in his Sermon on the Mount (see Matthew 5:1–12). So when we choose to enter into the forgiveness process

- We choose to do what God would have us do
- We choose to do what is very important for our physical and emotional health
- We choose to make our world a little more peaceful and loving

Chapter Three

Thirteen Truths to Remember About the Forgiveness Process

One reason that millions of people, including lots of good churchgoing people, remain stuck in a cycle of bitterness about some hurt or wrong done to them is that they do not believe in one or more of the following truths about forgiveness. (While the following list of truths about forgiveness may not be comprehensive, it does name the vast majority of the important truths that we need to remember as we seek to forgive a hurt.) As you read through the list you might want to ask yourself: Do I believe this?

1. Forgiveness is God's way of dealing with the hurt and wrong done to us. Seeking revenge or seeking to get even is the world's way.

13

Reflection Questions: Do you truly believe that forgiveness is *God's way* to deal with hurts and wrongs done to us? Or do you tend to believe that the way to deal with some hurts is to get even or ignore the hurt done to you?

2. Normally, people hurt us or do us wrong because they are immature, spiritually blind, weak, wounded, and imperfect like us, not because they are evil monsters or horrible, nasty people.

The late Father Anthony de Mello, S.J., popular writer and speaker, used to like to say, "people who hurt are asleep. If they were to wake up they would never behave like that." It seems de Mello was only echoing the words of Jesus. When dying on the cross, he said, "Father, forgive them; for they do not know what they are doing" (Luke 23:34). We might say: "Oh yes, they did know the evil thing that they did. Or at least their leaders did." Jesus would disagree with us.

In 2 Samuel 11:1–21 we read the story of how the great King David committed adultery and then arranged for a murder to cover up his sin. David was blind to both of these terrible sins and crimes until the prophet Nathan confronted him. We may wonder how David could be so blind to his sins. As we deal with the imperfections of others and ourselves, we must remember that sometimes very good people are capable of grievous sins or crimes. Also, all of us suffer periodically from spiritual blindness. Sometimes we suffer from having a deep need to believe that the one who hurt us "knew exactly what they were doing and fully intended to harm us." In rare cases this may be true, but usually it is not. Even when it seems to be true, we still have to admit that people act the way they do because they are spiritually asleep. For centuries, we as a nation were spiritually blind and asleep to the sin of racial prejudice.

Reflection Questions: If presently working through a hurt, what do you believe about your offender? Do you think he/she is a horrible, nasty person? or do you think he/she is an imperfect, weak, and spiritually asleep person who did you a terrible wrong?

3. Forgiveness of a hurt, especially a big hurt, usually takes time, patience, humility and lots of prayer.

We live in a society where we are used to getting quick results. When it comes to healing a wounded heart, there are usually no shortcuts or quick fixes. Just as we must be willing and very patient with our body as it recovers from major surgery, so must we be willing to be patient with our heart as it deals with a major hurt. To pray a few times and expect that the hurt will go away is unrealistic. Healing takes time and patience and much cooperation with God's grace. Of course, the pace of the healing will depend a great deal on the state of our psychological and spiritual health. For example, how easy or hard is it for us to name and express our feelings? How easy or hard is it for us to talk to God about the real stuff in our lives.

We need humility to help us know our need for God's

help. Those of us who suffer from pride and have big egos will, most likely, have a much more difficult time with the forgiveness process. We may have a difficult time admitting our need for God's help or counseling. On the other hand, if we are blessed with the virtue of humility we will have no problem getting down on our knees, admitting our powerlessness, and seeking God's help. Also, a recognition of our own imperfection and constant need for God's mercy will help us to minister mercy to those who have hurt us.

Reflection Questions: Do you agree that forgiveness takes time, patience, humility, and lots of prayer? Can you see where the presence of the sin of pride would be a huge block to anyone seeking to forgive life's hurts?

4. *Before we can forgive a hurt or wrong done to us, we usually will need to name, own, and give some expression to the feelings around the hurt, for example anger, disappointment, or a sense of betrayal.*

Often people make the mistake of beginning to pray for the grace to forgive a hurt prior to expressing the anger and other tough feelings they are experiencing due to the hurt. This piece of the process will be difficult for us if we have been taught to repress our feelings. While some of us may have no problem expressing our feelings, others of us may have a very difficult time doing it. We may have a difficult time simply admitting that we are as mad as hell at our offender. We may not want to admit that our offender actually did hurt us and make us feel very angry. We may have little or no experience expressing our anger. As a result, our tendency may be to say we are a "little upset" when in fact we may be very angry.

We can give expression to our anger in different ways. I often use my journal. I will use it to tell my offender exactly how I feel. If I need to use nasty or bad words to give vent to my feelings, I will do so. Usually, I feel better after I have vented. We can also vent to a friend.

Reflection Questions: How easy or hard is it for you to vent your anger? Do you tend to minimize it or exaggerate it? Can you see why it is important for us to be able to vent our anger before we can let it go.

5. *We usually need God's grace to help us let go of a big hurt.*

Remember the saying "To err is human. To forgive is divine." Forgiveness is a gift that we must frequently pray for. One reason many people do not make much progress with forgiveness is because they are unwilling to pray for God's help or because they do not know how to pray their way through a hurt. (More on this later.)

Reflection Questions: How easy is it for you to get down on your knees and seek the Lord's help? Or do you tend to fight life's battles with your own strength?

6. *Another reason we may not make much progress in our efforts to forgive is because deep down we do not want to let go.*

On the surface we may say or really believe that we want to forgive, but on a deeper level we may have a strong resistance to letting go of our hurt. Sometimes we may be aware that we have little or no desire to forgive. In this situation our prayer will be to have a strong desire to forgive.

Reflection Question: If presently you are seeking to forgive a hurt, do you think that you sincerely and truly desire to let it go?

7. *There is a difference between the forgiveness of a hurt and the healing of a hurt.*

Sometimes we may feel ill at ease because we still harbor negative feelings toward someone who has hurt us terribly in the past. We believe our negative feelings indicate that we do not have forgiveness in our heart. The hurt has been forgiven, but the wound has festered because the betrayal has not been healed. The point here is that we shouldn't necessarily conclude that we have not forgiven someone just because we still feel hurt and negative about what has happened. Forgiveness is primarily an *act of the will* and not a matter of feelings. If our negative feelings lead us to behave in negative ways, then we have every reason to believe that forgiveness has not taken place. Some hurts may have to be forgiven seventy times seven.

Reflection Question: Have you ever had the experience where you thought you had forgiven a hurt only to discover negative feelings emerging sometime later?

8. There is a difference between the forgiveness and the reconciliation of a hurt.

We can, with the grace of God, always forgive a hurt, but we cannot always reconcile a relationship. We can always forgive an offense that a person has committed against us, but we cannot always restore the relationship because the other person may not be interested. It only takes one person to forgive, but it takes two to reconcile a hurt. Jesus forgave his enemies (for example, the Pharisees), but obviously they had no interest in being reconciled with him.

Reflection Question: Have you ever confused the important distinction between the forgiveness and reconciliation of a hurt?

9. Sometimes the reason we have a difficult time forgiving others is because we have a difficult time forgiving ourselves.

The old saying "You cannot give what you haven't got," applies to forgiveness as much as to anything else. If we cannot *receive* from God and others the forgiveness they offer us, how can we *give* that same forgiveness to others? One big difference between Peter and Judas was that Peter was able to *accept* the forgiveness that Jesus offered, whereas Judas wasn't. Both had committed a grave offense against Jesus, and both were forgiven. But only one was able to *accept* the *gift* of forgiveness.

Reflection Questions: How easy or hard is it for you to forgive yourself? Can you see why it would be difficult to forgive others if we cannot forgive ourselves?

10. *Some hurts may be so serious that we will need a good counselor to help us work through the hurt.*

Sometimes it takes years for some people to talk about some deep hurt, for example rape. The hurt is so deep and painful that usually it cannot be dealt with alone. We would never even consider fighting a physical disease like cancer on our own. We would seek out the best help available to us. Why should it be any different when it comes to deep emotional hurts? A skilled counselor or spiritual guide can help us face and deal with the pain associated with deep emotional hurts. We would be wise to avail ourselves of such help.

Reflection Questions: Can you see how a good counselor or spiritual guide could help you as you struggle to forgive a hurt or wrong done to you? How willing would you be to go see a counselor or spiritual guide to help you deal with some hurt?

11. *It is important to remember that forgiveness of a hurt or wrong done to us is not a wimpy or weak response.*

This is especially important for us who may be a bit macho. The truth is that only people with strong spiritual fiber can forgive a hurt and let go of a hurt.

Reflection Questions: Do you tend to believe that forgiveness is a wimpy response to a hurt? Can you see why macho types of people might believe this?

12. It is important not to confuse the gospel call to forgive hurts with toleration of ongoing hurtful situations.

If we are in an abusive relationship we should do everything possible to either separate ourselves from the situation or confront the abuser. (More on this later.)

Reflection Question: Do you tend to overlook too easily and make excuses for the nasty behavior of others?

13. Remember that sometimes the truth hurts.

Sometimes the hurt that we may be dealing with is connected to facing the truth about some situation or ourselves, especially if the words spoken are said in a blunt fashion. You can be sure that many of the words Jesus spoke to the Pharisees and scribes deeply hurt and offended them (see Matthew 23). So sometimes our challenge is not so much to forgive some hurtful words spoken to us, but to face the truth of the words spoken to us. Needless to say, this demands a lot of humility and spiritual strength.

In a related way, we might say that people who tend

to be overly sensitive to what people say to them will have a lot more forgiving to do than people who are more spiritually mature or thick-skinned. When we are overly sensitive, we tend to be more frequently offended. Words spoken in jest are often interpreted as offensive.

Reflection Questions: Do you think that you tend to be overly sensitive to the remarks and actions of others? Do you think that sometimes you may have a difficult time facing the truth?

Chapter Four

Ten Obstacles to Forgiving Life's Hurts

We may wonder why Reggie Denny, Nancy Harris, and the others mentioned earlier were able to forgive a most horrible hurt, while some of us may be unable or unwilling to forgive a much lesser one. We may wonder why some good people cannot even get started with the forgiveness process. What blocks them or us from getting started?

Psychologists tell us that obstacles to forgiving a hurt are often unconscious. Hence the importance of naming a variety of obstacles that may be hindering us as we move through the forgiveness process. If, at this time, you are trying to forgive a hurt or wrong done to you, you can see if any of the following obstacles are present in your life.

1. Because of life's experiences, we may not be very forgiving. We may have been hurt a lot when we were

young or during our adult years. These experiences may have left us wounded or weakened in this area. We may have little experience of forgiveness. We may, in fact, have failed to actually accept forgiveness when offered. As a result we may have little forgiveness to offer to others. But then again through a miracle of grace, people who have had little forgiveness in their lives are able to forgive huge hurts.

2. We may feel strongly that our offender does not deserve our forgiveness. But, eventually we must ask: Do *we* deserve the forgiveness of others and especially do we deserve *God's* mercy for our many offenses against him? And let us not forget that even though we may believe that our offender does not deserve our forgiveness, *we* deserve to be free of all the resentment, pain, and stress that steals our joy because of a particular hurt.

3. Intellectually, we may feel consciously or unconsciously that Jesus is wrong on this issue. (I think many do.) We may feel some things should not be forgiven, such as acts of terrorism or some terrible wrong done to us.

4. Pride is a big obstacle for many people. Some of us may not be humble enough to get down on our knees and beg God to help us to do something that we may have absolutely no desire to do. Pride may also prevent us from accepting the sincere apologies of our offender.

5. Forgiving a hurt may seem like we are *minimizing* or *excusing* a hurt. It may seem like an act of weakness. Macho people do not like to come across as weak in any way. If we think forgiveness is an act of weakness, we should consider what Mahatma Gandhi once said: "The weak can never forgive. Forgiveness is an attribute of the strong."

6. Forgiveness involves facing emotions that most of us do not like to face and deal with, namely anger, hatred, and our need for revenge. If our tendency is to ignore our feelings, we are most likely going to have a very difficult time facing and dealing with tough feelings like anger, hatred, and revenge. We may not even want to admit that we have such feelings, let alone deal with them. If facing our feelings is an issue for us, remember that feelings are neither right nor wrong. Also, remember that Jesus, being fully human, experienced every human feeling.

7. We may fear that forgiveness would only leave us open to being hurt again. If we forgive our offender, he or she may interpret our mercy as weakness and hurt us again.

8. We may not even want to talk to God about the issue because we don't want to hear him say "forgive" or "let go." As a result we may even keep God at a distance. Of course, such a decision negatively impacts our *whole* relationship with him.

9. We may not be able to get beyond the anger and rage we feel that is related to the hurt. All we may be able to

think about is how we can get even with our offender. Of course, it's OK to be angry, we just need to decide *how long* we need to be angry. A year? Ten years? Twenty years? Keeping our anger alive is a decision to allow our offender to continue to control our emotions for years, or maybe for a lifetime. Do we really want to give our offender that much control and power over our lives emotionally and spiritually? Finally, we may feel (and this is nearly always unconscious) that our anger is all we have left when it comes to a particular relationship. If we let the anger go we may feel diminished, empty, and very powerless. Of course, our anger may be "righteous anger," the type Jesus showed when he cleansed the Temple (see John 2:13–17), the anger that drove Dr. King and Mothers Against Drunk Drivers to fight injustice. The anger we need to move past is the anger that makes us bitter and keeps us in a bad place emotionally and spiritually.

10. We may adopt what I call a "righteous victim stance." We may believe all the blame and wrong is with our offender. Of course, this *is* the situation sometimes, such as child abuse cases, but it is not the case most of the time. Sometimes we are so preoccupied with pointing out the splinter in our brother's eye that we cannot see that there might be a wooden beam in our own eye (see Matthew 7:1–5). When we are clearly in touch with our own sinfulness and our need for God's mercy, we will most likely find it easier to show mercy

to those who have hurt us. On the other hand, if we suffer from the spiritual disease of self-righteousness we will, most likely, be more resistant to forgiving others.

Reflection Question: Presently, if you are trying to forgive a hurt, which of the above obstacles to forgiveness might be operative in your life?

Chapter Five

How Prayer Can Help Forgive Life's Hurts

In this chapter we will look at how prayer can be a very helpful spiritual resource when we are struggling to forgive and reconcile a hurt. I will offer practical prayer suggestions that should help us

- To forgive another person, living or deceased
- To forgive God
- To forgive the Church
- To forgive ourselves

In some situations we may not need to pray to forgive or reconcile a hurt, but in many situations we will need divine assistance. Prayer is our way to tap into this assistance.

As stated earlier, before we begin to pray for the grace to forgive, it will be important to give expression to the feelings around the hurt or wrong done to us, such as rage, a desire to punish or get even, anger, or a sense of betrayal. I usually use a journal to vent my feelings. If I feel the person is a "rotten dirty skunk" I will say so. I will tell him or her (in my journal) how I feel like punching them. Naming, owning, and giving expression to our real feelings is a very important first step when it comes to dealing with life's hurts and injustices.

If the hurt is a big one (or even a small one) we may have little or no desire to forgive our offender. In this case our first prayer will express our anger, hate, and rage.

Prayer Suggestion 1:
Prayer of Rage

When we have been deeply hurt, we will most likely feel anger, rage, and hate. We want to get even and punish our offender. So our first prayer will need to give expression to our rage. It is likely that many of us may never have prayed a prayer of rage to God. It may be a new experience for us. The following is a sample prayer that we could use. Of course, it will be important to word each of the following prayer suggestions to suit your personality and the circumstances of your particular situation.

Jesus, I have absolutely no desire to forgive _____ _____ for the hurt and injustice he did to me. I am so angry with him. I hate his guts. I would even be happy if harm came his way. I cannot imagine

myself forgiving him. He is the scum of the earth.
I detest and despise him. I never want to see him
again.

As I said, most of us may never have prayed like that. In fact, we may feel it is wrong to say such things to God about another human being. If you are a little scandalized by the above prayer listen to what Jeremiah said to God about his enemies:

> *Let me put my case to you.*
> *Why does the way of the guilty prosper?*
> *Why do all who are treacherous thrive?*
> *Pull them out like sheep for the slaughter,*
> *and set them apart for the day of slaughter.*
>
> JEREMIAH 12:1, 3

Ouch, Jeremiah! Isn't that a bit over the top? We may not think so if we have experienced some terrible injustice or wrong.

When preaching about prayer, Martin Luther used to say, "don't lie to God." If our prayer is going to be real, it must express what we truly feel within. Many of the psalms are wonderful examples of honest speech to God in time of rage or depression. Listen to these words by an Israelite exile when he was experiencing oppression in Babylon.

O daughter Babylon, you devastator!
Happy shall they be who pay you back
what you have done to us!
Happy shall they be who take your little ones
and dash them against the rock!

PSALM 137:8–9

If we could not imagine ourselves speaking to God like that, I'm sure we can imagine some victims of terrorist attacks saying such words to God. Expressing out loud what we have judged to be unspeakable hurts can be a wonderful and freeing experience. Our reaction might be: "I said it and I already feel better."

Prayer Suggestion 2:
Prayer for the Desire to Forgive

Having expressed our rage to God and having expressed our disgust about our offender we will hopefully want to ask the Lord for help to move past our anger and outrage. A prayer that could help us at this stage might be

Jesus, you know the way I feel about _____.
You know my lack of desire to forgive. You know
that all I want to do is to get even with him.
But, I also know that holding onto a hardened,
unforgiving heart is bad for my body, mind, and
spirit. It hurts me more than it hurts my offender.
It also hurts my relationship with you.

Jesus, I admit my helplessness and power-lessness when it comes to even thinking about forgiving _____. But, I also know that all things are possible for those who cooperate with your grace. With Saint Paul, I believe that I can do all things in you who strengthens me. Empower me, Jesus, to do this work of forgiveness. Place within my heart the desire to forgive _____. I find it so hard to even make that request because my heart has so much venom toward _____. But I make the request however feebly hoping that you will give me the grace to do what I am powerless to do for myself.

Sometimes I will have to pray that prayer fervently *many* times before I will notice any desire to work through my hurt and anger. Just as physical therapy takes time, so it is with *spiritual* therapy. We have to stretch ourselves a lot emotionally and spiritually if we want God to melt a heart that is hardened. This may be the toughest step in the entire process. Millions of people choose not to even pray for the desire to forgive. If you find yourself stuck at this stage, I suggest you see a counselor or a spiritual guide.

Prayer Suggestion 3:
Prayer of Repentance

While there may be a rare situation where we are the totally innocent party and all the wrong is with the offending party, usually we have done something wrong either before, during, or after the event. For example, since the offense took place, we may have talked in an un-Christian way about our offender, not just to one person but to several. We may have slandered his or her good name. We may have exaggerated our account of what happened. If *we* have done wrong then *we* need to seek the Lord's forgiveness.

This piece of the forgiveness process is very challenging but also very helpful. It is very challenging because it asks us to move away from focusing on the sin or wrongdoing of our offender to focusing on our sin or wrongdoing. This step demands humility and a good bit of self-knowledge. As long as we keep the focus on what our offender did wrong we will not be able to forgive. But once we begin to focus on *our* need for forgiveness and mercy, we become much less self-righteous and condemning. This step is very helpful because it will, most likely, soften our hardened heart. Becoming deeply aware of our own need for mercy should ready our heart to show mercy to those who hurt us. At this stage our prayer could be something like this.

Jesus, forgive me for anything wrong I have said or done in this relationship. I have no problem telling others about how horrible _____ is but I have a big problem admitting my own wrongdoing. I ask your forgiveness for the way I have spoken in an un-Christian way about _____.

Now take a moment to ponder other ways you may have sinned or done wrong before, during, or after the hurt or injustice occurred.

After naming the specific wrongs you may have done, ask the Lord's forgiveness. Then you might add

Jesus, I accept your mercy and thank you for the countless number of times you have forgiven me. Grace me with the strength and power to forgive _____.

Prayer Suggestion 4: Prayer for the Offender

To get some sense of where a person is in the forgiveness process I will sometimes ask, "Can you pray for him?" If the response is "no," I then realize that the hurt person still has a ways to go. The thought of praying for one who deeply hurt us is repulsive to many people. It is like wishing them well, when all that we may want to do is wish them evil.

I have personally found my decision to begin to pray for my offender to be very helpful. Invariably, it leads to a softening of my heart. Also, as we stretch ourselves to do what we may find repulsive, God will usually create in us a new heart, a heart more like his, a heart more open to forgiving what seems unforgivable. At this stage we may begin to experience the miracle of forgiveness—the miracle of wanting to let go of something that we had previously held on to as if it were a precious jewel. A simple prayer at this stage might be

Lord, you created _____ good just like you created me good.
You love _____ just as you love me with all my faults and weaknesses.
You know I do not love _____ very much at this time, but you do love him or her.
Share with me your love for _____.
Also, God, I ask you to bless this scoundrel. Sometimes I, too, am a scoundrel and in need of your blessing.

If we fervently pray the above prayer or a similar one over and over we will most likely discover that God is creating a new heart in us.

Prayer Suggestion 5:
Prayer for Deliverance From an Evil Spirit

In his book *Healing in the Spirit* (Liguori Publications, 2003), Father Jim McManus, C.Ss.R., has a chapter titled "Breaking the Bondage" in which he tells two remarkable stories of two good Catholic women who very much wanted to forgive a big hurt, but felt powerless to do so. Father Jim writes

Sometimes the barrier to inner healing may be the action of the evil spirit. This does not necessarily imply that the person who is the victim of the evil spirit's action is bad or evil. It may mean simply that while the person was very hurt or weak the evil spirit took advantage and used the hurt or weakness to form a bondage.

While I was on a parish mission in the west of Scotland a lady came to see me during a house Mass. Everyone at the Mass was coming to confession. She came in and said, "I can't go to confession, but I would like to talk." I presumed that she could not come to confession because she may have been married outside the Church. "Oh no," she said, "I can't forgive, so there is no point in me going to confession."

She then told me her sad story. Her only son was serving a life sentence for the murder of a young man. She was convinced that this young

man and his family goaded her son beyond en-
durance and that he had no intention of killing.
But he was found guilty and sentenced. Now her
heart was full of hatred. "I have no peace," she
said, "because I hate them and I can't forgive
them." I asked her if she would like to forgive
and she responded immediately, "I would love
to. It is like a cold stone in my heart."

She was a good woman, a devout Catholic,
I saw her at all the services of the mission. I had
not realized until then she was not coming to the
sacraments. Here was a very clear case of a woman deeply desiring to do the Christ-like thing and
forgive and not being able to do it. Through the
tragic killing on her son's part she now found her-
self bonded through hatred with the family whose
son he killed. She was in real bondage. She was
not free.

I explained to her that Jesus would set her
free and give her the power to forgive. As I was
praying with her I bound that evil sprit of hatred
in the name of Jesus and silently commanded it
to depart and never return. I then asked the Lord
to fill her with his forgiving love. The hatred and
coldness in her heart immediately left her and she
knew she had forgiven them. During that house
Mass she received Holy Communion for the first
time in years with great joy.

It seems clear from this story that when we allow our hearts to become hardened and filled with hatred toward someone, we open ourselves to allowing an evil spirit to enter our life and make forgiveness very difficult, if not impossible, without divine intervention.

If you are trying to forgive a big hurt and all you feel is animosity and hatred, you may need a prayer for deliverance to break the bondage of an evil spirit. You may want to ask a priest who is open to such a prayer to pray with you. Or you may want to seek out a layperson with experience in the healing ministry to pray with you.

Chapter Six

Moving Through Forgiveness to Reconciliation

While the gospels call us to forgive every hurt and wrong done to us, it does not call us to be reconciled with everyone who offends us. Obviously, reconciliation is not possible if our offender is not sorry for his wrongdoing and has no desire to be reconciled with us. Also, if we had little or no relationship with our offender prior to when he offended us, we will not need to develop a relationship after we have forgiven him. The late Pope John Paul II forgave the man who tried to assassinate him. He even visited him in his prison cell. But after that we can assume that he did not seek to continue a relationship with him.

In many cases, we are called to not only forgive the person who offended us, but to also reconcile with him. This would obviously be true in the case of family relationships. In a parish setting it is also desirable that all who participate in the Eucharist are in good relationship with one another. In the gospel, Jesus speaks the following challenging words to us:

> *When you are offering your gift at the altar,*
> *if you remember that your*
> *brother or sister has something against you,*
> *leave your gift there before the altar and go;*
> *first be reconciled to your brother or sister,*
> *and then come and offer your gift.*
>
> MATTHEW 5:23–24

But then again, someone in your family or parish circle may have deeply hurt you and have no desire to express contrition or to relate to you. In this case all we can do is try to forgive our offender and when we meet him, be as Christ-like as we can.

Using Our Imagination to Prepare for a Reconciliation Meeting

Assuming that we desire to be reconciled with our offender, and assuming that our offender may also desire to be reconciled with us, we could draw on the gift of our imagination to help us.

Our imagination is one of the wonderful faculties that God has bestowed on us. It can serve us very well in our relationship with God. Saint Ignatius, founder of the Jesuits, urged his followers to use their imagination when reading the gospel stories. He would tell his listeners, "See yourself in the story, be a part of the crowd, be this or that character."

Unfortunately, some of us too often use our imagination to our disadvantage rather than to our advantage. Sometimes we allow it to "run away with us." When we are hurt, we allow our imagination to do us a disservice when we exaggerate the hurt, especially when we attribute all kinds of ill will and bad motives to the person who hurt us. We make him or her out to be some kind of terrible monster. Because we are morally and spiritually asleep, we return hurt for hurt.

The following is a suggestion on how to use our imagination to let go of a hurt. Once we have decided that we are ready to engage in the exercise, we should tailor the following suggestion to fit our circumstances and temperament, remembering that some of us are very emotional and expressive, while others are not.

Imagine Jesus and the person you wish to forgive talking in the sanctuary area of the church. You enter the front door and notice them. You wait and watch them chatting. When you are ready, you walk up the aisle to them. Both of them stop talking and begin to turn toward you. When you arrive, you say "Hi." Then you speak to the one you wish to forgive and be reconciled with:

"_____, I have been asking Jesus to help me forgive you for the hurt you inflicted on me.

I think I am now ready to forgive you. Also, I wish to ask you to forgive me for the very negative thoughts and feelings I have harbored toward you since the day you hurt me."

You may now wish to shake hands with or hug the other person. (You can also shake Jesus' hand or hug him and tell him thanks for helping you with all this.) You can do that even if you know the other person doesn't wish to be reconciled with you.

In the above scene, we are simply trying to act out a forgiveness and reconciliation scenario: an imaginative meeting that might help us to forgive and let go of the hurt done to us.

If we have never done imaginative prayer, we might immediately judge that it is not for us, but don't judge it without trying it a few times. Many of us can testify to the positive benefit of the above exercise in the forgiveness-and-reconciliation process. If we cannot forgive or be reconciled with someone in our *imagination*, we can be sure we are not ready to do it in reality. This type of exercise can prepare us for a real flesh-and-blood meeting, assuming one is desired. In any case, the use of our imagination in this way will be very helpful.

Using a Letter to Initiate a Reconciliation Meeting

The decision to take an active step to be reconciled with someone who has hurt us or someone whom we have hurt has some risks. First, the other person may reject our offer to meet. Second, if a meeting happens, it may be unsuccessful and add only more fuel to the fire. But life is full of risks and anytime we risk rejection in the interest of healing relational hurts, we are doing the work of Christ.

A simple and effective way to initiate reconciliation is through a well-written, conciliatory letter. Through means of a letter, we can express sorrow for our part in the wounded relationship and we can create a fertile ground for reconciliation to happen. Needless to say, if we write with a judgmental tone we will certainly set ourselves up for failure and only cause a greater gap in the relationship. A letter may be as simple as this:

Dear _____,
I have been reflecting on and praying about the events that caused alienation between us. I feel bad about the distance in our relationship. I also feel sorry for any words and actions of mine that contributed to this rift and hurt. If you are interested in getting together to talk or let bygones be bygones, I would welcome that.

As you can see, such a letter is very conciliatory in tone and certainly does everything possible to create an atmosphere of reconciliation.

The positive thing about using a letter is that is allows us to say what it is we need to say without getting flustered. It also gives the other person space to respond to our outreach. There is a very good chance that our conciliatory letter will create a desire in the other person to meet and reconcile with us.

To Talk or Not to Talk About the Hurt

If both parties agree to meet, a decision to talk or not to talk about the hurt will need to be made. Both parties may need to talk about what happened or they may not. Or one party may need to talk and the other may not. If both parties are genuinely willing to let bygones be bygones, then no rehashing of the issues is needed. But on the other hand, a good open conversation may be very helpful. False perceptions and misunderstandings may be cleared up with the result that a new and better relationship is created.

If a conversation is to occur about some hurt or conflict, both parties will need to be mature and skillful enough to

- Listen to the other in a non-defensive way.
- Admit where they may have done wrong and ask for forgiveness. Any genuine declaration of forgiveness

will wear thin if it is not accompanied by a change of heart, both in the forgiver and the forgiven. In other words, it must cost something if it is to have any lasting effect.

- Stand their ground if that seems the right thing to do. This is especially important if our tendency is to wimp out and to take the blame for conflicts.

If we decide to have a conversation, we should ideally prepare our mind and heart with prayer. Ask the Holy Spirit to help both parties to listen well, admit wrong, and stand our ground when appropriate.

If the reconciliation encounter goes well, give thanks to the Lord. If it doesn't go well, seek his help about the right thing to do. Perhaps more time is needed to work through the feelings around the issue. Perhaps a third party or counselor is needed to facilitate a meeting.

Deepening Forgiveness and Reconciliation

When two people are married, they vow to love and cherish each other until death do them part. That first decision to love will need to be renewed again and again by countless other decisions to love. Otherwise, the decision will gradually diminish and will not be expressed in loving deeds. In the same way, we can also say that the initial act of forgiveness and reconciliation will need to be ratified by other acts of love. Of course, this cannot happen when only forgiveness but not reconciliation has taken place.

A great danger in the forgiveness and reconciliation process is that even though we make the right move, we do so only *externally* or on the surface. Internally, however, we may be only seeking to look good in our own eyes and in the eyes of our offender by saying all the right words: "I'm sorry; forgive me; I forgive you." Yet we may continue to harbor resentments and grudges in our heart. We *say* we are sorry or that we forgive, but deep down we aren't and we don't. Because of this, sooner or later the resentments will show their ugly head in our words and behavior.

It would be much more honest for us to be open and say: "I forgive you, but I am still struggling with many negative feelings. You'll have to be patient with me." By saying this, we avoid sending out a conflicting message: *saying* one thing with our mouths and *doing* another with our actions.

Our forgiveness and reconciliation are genuine only when we accompany them with genuine acts of love. Of course, the nature of the relationship will dictate how much follow-up work is in order. If we had little or no relationship with the other person before the conflict, then perhaps we need not follow up with acts of love. In this situation, all we need to do is to check that our heart remains free of bitterness and resentment.

At this stage of the process, our prayer will consist

mainly of asking God to protect and deepen the forgiveness and reconciliation he has granted us. Satan's work is to divide and tear down. He doesn't give up easily. Even after reconciliation has happened, Satan will try to fill our heart with old and new resentments. Therefore, we should pray:

Lord, I thank you for the reconciliation that has taken place between _____ and me. You know that our hearts are very fragile and vulnerable. Please protect our hearts from all negative feelings, words, and deeds and enable us to keep our reconciliation intact.

Chapter Seven

Forgiving a Deceased Person

When a loved one dies, many people have to face what is called "unfinished business." If the death was sudden, there was probably no opportunity to say goodbye. Survivors may feel guilty that they didn't push their loved one to go to a doctor, that they somehow neglected to care for him or her, or that some conflict was never dealt with, forgiven, and reconciled.

On the other hand, people in grief ministry tell us that survivors sometimes feel angry at their loved one for dying, for not taking care of their health, for keeping them in a very dependent relationship, for not telling them about financial matters, or for confining their social life to one or two friends. Survivors sometimes have a hard time allowing negative feelings to surface. They may feel guilty about having such feelings and they do not know what to do with them. Many think nothing can be done since their loved one is now deceased. The good news is that much can be done. Unfinished business can be processed, forgiven, and reconciled. As Christians, we believe in life after death. The Preface of a Catholic Funeral Mass states:

> Lord, for your faithful people life is changed,
>   not ended.
> When the body of our earthly dwelling lies
>   in death
> we gain an everlasting dwelling place in heaven.

We can still communicate with those who have gone before us and trust that they are aware of what we are saying to them.

Exercise 1:
Write a Farewell Letter

The purpose of this letter is to help us deal with any guilty feelings or unfinished business that we may have concerning our relationship with our deceased loved one. Also, if we never had the opportunity to say goodbye, this letter can also serve such a purpose. Before writing, remember that the loved one is now in a new, transformed state of being. He or she has a much greater capacity to give and receive love, to forgive and be forgiven. If the person were here on earth, we may rightly wonder how he or she may receive and respond to our letter. But now we can feel certain that our letter will be received with openness and that the response will be coming from someone who is now totally transformed.

When writing, we should pour out our heart, expressing all the feelings and emotions we are experiencing, saying all those tender things we often wanted to say but didn't. If we feel guilty about anything, we should seek forgiveness and believe that we are receiving it. If we feel odd about writing such a letter, we should know that this is normal. But we must not let these feelings stop us from doing what many, many people have found to be tremendously helpful and healing. Of course, it may take some time in the grieving process before we are ready to write such a letter. That's okay. Remember to take time and be patient. But also remember that no progress is made without a decision to stretch ourselves to do what we do not feel like doing.

The second part of this exercise involves imagining the response our loved one might write to us. We should ask the Holy Spirit to help us write such a letter, recalling once again that our beloved deceased is now in a new and transformed state of being that we will never fully understand until we ourselves enter into eternity. We know that the letter coming back to us will be full of tenderness, love, and care.

Finally, when we have finished writing the letter, we can imagine ourselves in the presence of Jesus and our loved one. Say whatever needs to be said. Embrace Jesus. Then embrace the loved one and let him/her go to Jesus.

Obviously, such a scenario may be very emotional, and it may take a good amount of time before we can deal with it. But with proper concentration on our part, we can manage it.

Exercise 2:
A Letter Dealing With Hurt and Resentment

This exercise is aimed at helping us deal with the anger and hurt we may feel toward a loved one who has died. The letter outlines the hurts suffered by the person who is still alive. The first step is to give ourselves the permission to feel hurt and angry. Remembering feelings are neither right nor wrong. It is very important to our emotional well-being that we express them in appropriate ways. Then, we should write a letter stating exactly how we feel, resisting the temptation to minimize our hurt. We might begin in the following way, tailoring the letter to fit the circumstances of our situation:

> *Dear* _____,
> *Recently, I have become aware of how angry and resentful I am about some things that happened between us while you were alive—some things you said and did....*

You can now take time to state exactly how you feel and list the things you are hurt and angry about. For example, you may have been kept in the dark about financial matters; you may have been very restricted socially because your deceased partner was very private or he or she did not want to travel. You can express the anger you may feel about being controlled and the anger you may feel at yourself for allowing yourself to be controlled. It is important that we, too, recognize how we may have contributed to our unhappy situation by constantly submitting to our spouse's every whim and wish.

Performing this helpful exercise may be difficult for two reasons: First, we may feel disloyal about thinking and writing negative things about our deceased loved one. Second, we may have little or no experience in dealing with our anger. Over the years we may have learned only too well how to hold our angry and hurt feelings in check. We may even think that writing a negative letter would be sinful. The truth is that writing such a letter will most likely be a very healing and helpful exercise. Again, we need to remember that growth invariably means stretching ourselves beyond our comfort zone.

The next step will depend on whether or not we want to forgive the hurts and wrongs done to us. If we do not, then hopefully we will be open to going through the steps suggested earlier. If we are open to forgiving our loved one, then state that in the letter.

Then you may want to take time to imagine how your loved one may respond to you. If you decide to take this step, do remember that your loved one is now a new and transformed person. He or she will have a much greater capacity to express love and tenderness than they did while here on earth. You can ask the Holy Spirit to help you write the kind of response letter your loved one might write to you. To help you get started, imagine the kind of letter you would write if you were the deceased one and now totally transformed.

Finally, we can imagine ourselves in the presence of Jesus and our loved one. Say whatever needs to be said. Embrace Jesus. Embrace the loved one and let him or her go to Jesus.

If there is a great deal of hurt inside us, we will most likely need the help of a counselor to process it. Also, check to see if your local church or hospice centers have support groups for people who have lost a loved one. Many people find such groups to be an excellent way to process the hurt connected with someone who is now deceased.

Chapter Eight

Forgiving God

Some people are shocked and even scandalized when they hear about our possible need to forgive God. They exclaim, "How could we be in a situation to forgive God? After all he and his ways are perfect." While it is indeed true to say that God and his ways are perfect, it is also true to say that his ways may also deeply hurt us and cause us to distance ourselves from him. When we pray for a sick child to be healed and he isn't, we may consciously, or often unconsciously, distance ourselves from God. The same may happen when we pray for a marriage to be saved or for a spouse to change his or her wayward ways. We pray for protection against a hurricane and all we have is destroyed. We wonder why a good and all-powerful God could allow such terrible things to happen to good people. Coming to terms with unanswered prayer and destruction in our lives or in the lives of our loved ones, can be very difficult even for people with deep faith.

How to Respond

When we experience God not answering our prayer or when we experience bad things happening to us or to others, the *worst* thing we can do is to break our relationship with God or distance ourselves from him. When we do this, we hand Satan a victory. The devil's plan is to always use the bad things in life to weaken or destroy our relationship with God. Unfortunately, this happens all too often. I'm sure all of us can understand why some people who experience terrible things might conclude that God doesn't care about them. After all, he is the one with all the power. Why would he not intervene?

When bad things happen to us or our loved ones, the best thing to do for our relationship with God is to let him know exactly how we feel. This is what the psalmists and other great figures in the Old Testament did. When God acted, Israel did not remain silent. They let God know exactly how they felt about his action or lack thereof. The following are some examples of people sharing their honest feelings and thoughts with God in a time of darkness. Each of them could have broken their relationship with God or mouthed rote prayers. Instead they chose to stay in a relationship with God and tell him exactly how they felt. Let us begin with words from Psalm 22:1, 2, words used by Christ on the cross when he may have felt abandoned by God in his hour of darkness and pain:

> *My God, my God, why have you forsaken me?*
> *O my God, I cry by day,*
> *but you do not answer;*
> *and by night, but find no rest.*

In Psalm 44:23, 24, we hear these words:

> *Why do you sleep, O Lord?*
> *Why do you hide your face?*
> *Why do you forget our affliction*
> *and oppression?*

During his time of spiritual darkness, Job spoke these words:

> *I was at ease, and [God] broke me in two;*
> *he seized me by the neck and*
> *dashed me to pieces;*
> *he set me up as his target;*
> *his archers surround me.*

16:12–13

If and when we feel God has abandoned us and allowed evil to triumph, we could express our anger or disappointment in the following way:

> *God, I'm so mad with you.*
> *I'm sick and tired of people telling me how good*
> *you are.*

If you are so all-loving, how come you allow
natural disasters to kill thousands of people
and throw millions of lives into chaos.
I see so many bad people get away with murder
while many of your dedicated servants get beat up.
What kind of God are you?

Most likely, few if any of us were taught to speak to God like that. It may be safe to say that we would have been told that it is sinful to speak to him in such a disrespectful way. Some of us may *still* believe this. Yet, if we sometimes feel like giving God a piece of our minds, we should go ahead and do so. We can be certain he can handle it. We can also be certain that God will be happier with our heartfelt prayer of anger than with our rote prayers that do not express how we truly think and feel.

Spiritual guides frequently remind us that one reason why our relationship with God may feel lifeless is because we have stopped expressing our true feelings about the real stuff going on in our lives and in our world. We nearly always feel better emotionally and spiritually when we give true expression to what is really going on within us. Failure to do so only creates a distance between God and us. Consciously or unconsciously, bad feelings about God and his workings in the world will fester within us.

Just as it takes us some time to work through our anger with another who has hurt us, it may take us some time to work through our anger with God. That is okay and normal. But, of course, we must ideally keep relating to God even if it is with anger. If it seems we are not able to work through the anger, it would be good for us to see a spiritual guide. Also at this time we may want to pray in the following way:

God, even though I am as mad as hell with you,
I do not want to stay that way
because it is destructive to our relationship
and not helpful to my well-being.
So help me Lord to get through this difficult time,
protect me from the workings of the devil
who always wants to use bad situations
to alienate me from you.

Even though at times we may feel very alienated from God and mad at him, he is in truth the one who knows us best and loves us most. He proved this when he decided to become one of us and when he was willing to die a cruel death for our salvation. Having said this, I realize very much that it has to be very difficult for some people who have been handed such trials to keep faith in a God who loves us very much. When we feel distant from God, when we are angry with him we are very much engaged in spiritual warfare (see Ephesians 6:10–17). The powers of darkness are trying every trick in the book to make us believe that God does not care about us, while the Holy Spirit is trying very much to help us to see God's presence even in the midst of our tribulations.

Also, when God seems aloof, distant, uncaring, or

even cruel, it may be very helpful for us to turn our minds and hearts to Jesus, God in human flesh. Is the God we see at work in Jesus distant, aloof, and uncaring in the face of human suffering? Even a brief look at the gospels, shows us a God deeply involved with people's trials and tribulations. The God we see at work in Jesus never walks away from people's pain and suffering. When he hears of Lazarus' death, he weeps and is deeply moved (see John 11:33–35). This is hardly an image of a God who doesn't care. Rather it is an image of a God who deeply cares about people and their pain. As it is commonly said, "Jesus came not to solve the problems of suffering, but to fill it with his presence." We can certainly see the truth of this saying as we look at the life and ministry of Jesus. It will always be a great mystery why a good and loving God allows so much suffering in our world. But, if we keep our eyes focused on Jesus, we would never conclude that God doesn't care about our pain or other people's pain.

We may also want to consider seeking the help of Mary, our Blessed Mother. She surely had every reason to believe that God abandoned her and cared nothing about her as she watched the enemies of her son treat him so badly. Mary continued to believe in God and his care for her even as he allowed the horrific things to happen to her innocent son. If you are a Catholic, consider praying and reflecting on The Sorrowful Mysteries of the rosary (The Agony in the Garden, The Scourging at the Pillar, The Crowning with Thorns, The Carrying of the Cross, and The Crucifixion and Death).

Chapter Nine

Forgiving Religious and Secular Institutions

Many people are hurt by institutions—religious and secular. Unfortunately some Catholics have been badly and even cruelly treated by priests and by religious Sisters and Brothers during their school years. The report of sex scandals is one of the worst chapters in the history of our Church in the United States. Other people were hurt when the Church was not present to them and their family in a time of great need. Some people who worked for the Church may have been very unfairly and unjustly treated by the Church leaders. People have also been badly hurt and wronged by other institutions. They may have been unjustly treated by unscrupulous employers. They may have been fired for unjust reasons. Many have lost their retirement pension. Some people have suffered so badly at the hands of religious and secular institutions that one wonders how they could ever come to peace with the hurt and injustice done to them.

What Might Help Us Forgive What Seems Unforgivable

In his book *The Art of Forgiving* (Ballantine Books, 2006), Lewis B. Smedes writes, "Remember that forgiving was invented precisely as a remedy for wounds that intolerable wrongs leave with us." Smedes is reminding us that forgiveness is the medicine God offers to heal the wounds and scars left in us because of terrible hurts and wrongs done to us. As stated earlier, to choose not to do the difficult work of forgiveness is to choose to allow our offender to *continue* to wound us and have incredible power over our emotional and spiritual lives. So we enter the forgiveness process because we care deeply about our own emotional and spiritual welfare and because we do not want our offender to go on hurting us and of course because Jesus calls us to forgive even those who have grievously hurt us.

As we take the steps to forgive representatives of religious and secular institutions that failed and wronged us, remember that it is entirely appropriate to be very angry with the person(s) who did us wrong. Even after we have decided to forgive, it is normal to be mad at our offender. But it is not appropriate or right to *hate* our offender. Lewis Smedes goes on:

The enemy of forgiving is hate, not anger. Anger is aimed at what persons do. Hate is aimed at persons. Anger keeps bad things from happening again to you. Hate wants bad things to happen to our offender. Anger is the positive power that pushes us toward justice. Hate, by that token, is the negative force that pushes us toward vengeance. Anger is one of love's good servants. Hate serves nobody well. So if you get angry when you remember what he or she did to you, it does not mean that you have not forgiven him. It only means that you get mad when people do bad things to you.

Each of us must decide what steps will help us to move through the forgiveness process. Personally, the thing that helps me the most is believing that my offender is not some monster (even if he or she did a monstrous wrong), but rather my offender is spiritually asleep. Our offender could be a very well-educated or a religious person, a CEO, a bishop, or someone that we believe should have known better. But the truth is that even very well-educated and religious people including clergy can be very asleep spiritually. If he or she were spiritually awake they would not do the horrible thing they did.

Suggested Steps

- Give expression to the feelings you have around your particular hurt. Perhaps write a letter to the one who hurt you and acted unjustly toward you. You will need to decide whether or not you want to mail the letter. It may be helpful to do so.

- Bring the hurt and injustice to prayer. If your hurt has to do with the Church you might say something like "Jesus, I am so mad with this Church of yours and especially with _____ *(name the representatives of the Church who did you wrong)*. Let me tell you how poorly they represented you when dealing with me (or with some family member)." If the hurt took the form of emotional, physical, sexual, or spiritual abuse you will most likely need some help from a skilled counselor trained to deal with your hurt and abuse.

- Having taken time to give expression to your feelings and brought them to prayer, a next helpful step might be to go visit a priest and share your hurt. If you decide to take this step, be sure that you choose a priest who can empathize with your hurt. The last thing you need is to meet with a priest who will become defensive and who is unable or unwilling to feel your pain and express apologies for the Church that so badly failed you. During my years as a priest, God has used me many times to help people deal with a hurt or wrong inflicted upon them by representatives or members of the Church. So a session with a cler-gyperson can be very helpful.

As you struggle to deal with the hurt and injustice, the following prayer to Jesus might help:

Jesus, I know that you also suffered much at the hands of religious and secular authorities.
They rejected you, twisted your words, and frequently mistreated you.
Yet somehow you forgave them.
You know I have a hard time letting go of the hurt I feel toward our Church.
Yet despite her many weaknesses and failures to care for us, your people, she is the imperfect instrument you have chosen to continue your work on earth.
Help me to let go of the hurt I feel toward our Church (name the persons who hurt you).
I want to do this because you tell us over and over in your word to forgive.

If the hurt you are dealing with has to do with a secular institution, the above prayer will need to be adjusted. In fact, you may be better served by using the prayer suggestions on pages 30–39. In addition you may need to re-read what I said about the various obstacles that may hinder you from forgiving a hurt or injustice (pages 23–27).

Finally, remember that even though we are always

called to forgive life's hurts, we are not called to be quiet about wrongdoing. Dr. Martin Luther King, Jr., forgave those who physically assaulted him and his family, but yet he continued to speak out against racial injustice. If there is something wrong going on in the Church, we should speak out—but to the proper authorities.

Chapter Ten

Forgiving Yourself

In the forgiveness process, many people discover that forgiving ourself can be a very difficult thing to do. The following are some examples of the things that people may have a difficult time forgiving themselves for:

- Killing of another. The killing may be intentional, such as war or abortion or unintentional, in the case of a car or gun accident.
- Parental issues: guilt about neglect of children due to work, poor health, or preoccupation with one's own needs or wants or physical, emotional, or sexual abuse of children by oneself or one's spouse.
- Marital issues: infidelity or other forms of mean and unloving behavior toward one's spouse.
- Work issues: the bad way we treated an employee, employer, or coworker.
- Lies and half-truths that did serious damage to the good name of another.

- For failing to act or speak up in a particular situation, for example when a coworker was being very unjustly treated.

Sometimes our guilt flows from a perfectionist spirit that blames us for not being the perfect daughter or son, spouse, parent, friend, or church member. Some examples:

- When adult children do not practice their faith or when they join another church or adopt a life style or a value system very different from the one they were raised in. Parents often blame themselves even though they tried to set a good example for their children.
- Adult children often feel a lot of guilt for placing their parent(s) in a nursing home—even when it is apparent to everyone that they can no longer care for them.
- For not caring better for a sick loved one.

Steps Toward Self-forgiveness

- If one has clearly engaged in immoral or un-Christian behavior, the first step is to pray for the grace of *true contrition*. When one has been granted this grace then one should bring the sin to the sacrament of reconciliation if one belongs to a church family that has this sacrament. Hearing a priest speak the words of absolution can be most helpful to us when we have a difficult time forgiving ourselves for our faults and failings. Without true contrition for the wrong we did we have no business forgiving ourselves. Also, if our sin involved stealing money and property from someone, we should do everything possible to make restitution. If this is not possible we should make a generous donation to charity.

- When possible we should also ask the forgiveness of the person(s) we harmed by our sin or wrong behavior. Of course, the person(s) we wronged may or may not be ready to forgive us. Usually the victim's willingness to forgive us our wrongdoing will help us to forgive ourselves, but sometimes it may not. When the one we offended is not willing to forgive us, our attempt to forgive ourselves will, most likely, be more difficult.

Three Questions

Question 1: What if we cannot forgive ourselves even though we believe that God and the victim have forgiven us?

This is sometimes the case of a spouse who knew her husband was abusing their children but she did nothing to stop it. Frequently, such a person will need the help of counseling and prayer therapy to help them internalize the mercy that has already been given. Also, we need to ask ourselves who are we not to forgive ourselves if we believe God and the one we wronged has forgiven us? Failure to forgive ourselves when we are truly contrite for what we did is a form of self-hatred, which is very destructive to our ongoing personal and spiritual growth.

Question 2: What if we are truly sorry for the wrong we did but have a difficult time believing God has forgiven us?

We would do well to spend time with Scripture texts that speak of God's mercy. For example:

- Psalm 51 is an act of contrition attributed to King David. This is the prayer he prayed after he repented for the sin of adultery and murder.

Luke's Gospel is sometimes called the "gospel of mercy" because it has several stories that speak of God as rich in mercy. For example:

- Luke 7:36–48: Jesus shows mercy to the penitent woman.
- Luke 15: Three parables on divine mercy. When the Pharisees accused Jesus of being too soft on sin, he told them three stories to help them understand why he welcomed sinners and ate with them. A good exercise for us is to imagine ourselves as the prodigal son or daughter being embraced by our loving father (verse 20).
- Luke 23:34: Jesus forgives those responsible for his cruel sufferings and execution.
- Luke 23:39–43: Jesus forgives and promises paradise to the so-called "good thief."

Prayerful reflection on the above texts should be very helpful as we seek to believe in and accept God's mercy for even the most heinous wrong or crime.

Question 3: What if we are truly contrite and believe God has forgiven us but our victim doesn't even want to talk to us let alone forgive us?

If we are truly contrite for what we did wrong and ask God's forgiveness we can indeed believe that God has forgiven us even if the one we hurt or wronged will not forgive us. Our sincere contrition for our wrongdoing and God's mercy is what Lewis Smedes calls our "permission slip" to forgive ourselves. While we may understand why the person we wronged has a very difficult time forgiving us, we should not hold ourselves in bondage for his/her failure to forgive us. God would not want us to do this. The victims of the good thief on the cross most likely did not forgive him for his wrongdoings, but Jesus did forgive him and that made all the difference.

Dealing With a Perfectionistic Spirit

Sometimes a big obstacle to forgiving ourselves for our faults and failings is the presence within us of a strong perfectionist spirit or voice. The presence of such a voice will also make it very difficult for us to believe in God's love and mercy. This is the inner voice that harshly condemns us for not being perfect. It holds up before us an unattainable standard. Its favorite Scripture is of course the verse that has Jesus saying "be perfect, therefore, as your heavenly Father is perfect" (Matthew 5:48)—a verse that some Scripture scholars translate as "be you whole as our heavenly Father is whole."

Psychologists tell us that the root course of this perfectionistic voice is a strict upbringing during which we received a long list of what good boys and girls "should" be. For example: "you should never get angry," "boys should never cry," "you should not have impure thoughts," or "you should always get A's at school." Usually God's love and mercy were not emphasized. Instead children mainly heard of God's judgment and punishment for those who failed to (rigidly) follow his ways.

Frequently, the "list of shoulds" (not all of which were bad) were internalized and became like "parental tapes" in our psyche. They told us what was right and wrong and exerted a great influence over our lives. If our upbringing was morally very strict and rigid we may have developed a scrupulous conscience, which left us feeling we were always sinning and that God was a punishing God and not very loving. While no one may have actually said to us that we had to be perfect to deserve God's love and mercy. We may have mistakenly come to that unfortunate conclusion—a conclusion that would make it very difficult in the future for us to forgive ourselves and to believe in God's love and mercy.

All of us who in childhood were so unfortunate to receive a *lot* of "shoulds" from parental and authority figures were set up to *not* enjoy life too much. We can see from the previous paragraphs the importance of learning to deal with a perfectionistic inner voice if we carry one within us.

Three Suggestions

- Take time to read Scriptures that speak of God's love and mercy. I have already listed several that speak to us of God's mercy. The following are some Scriptures that speak of his love: Isaiah 43:4, Hosea 11:1–5, John 15:9, 1 John 4:8–10, and Romans 5:5, 8:31–39. Slowly reading and meditating on the above Scriptures should help us to hear God say to us, "I love you and you are very precious in my eyes. I love you even when you do wrong. There is *nothing* you can do to diminish the love I have for you." Internalizing this Good News may take time especially if for years we only believed how *unworthy* we were of God's love and mercy.

- Become aware of the inner voice sometimes also called our "inner critic" and learn to gently but firmly speak back to it. Many of us are unaware of our inner critic that loves to tell us how we are not measuring up. As we become aware of our inner critic we can speak back to it as we would to a domineering outer voice or critic that seeks to put us down and tell us how undeserving we are of good things. In order to deal effectively with a domineering person in our lives, we have to learn to assert ourselves; otherwise we will be bullied, intimidated, and walked all over.

The same principle applies when it comes to dealing with a domineering inner voice. We may say something like "Yes, I have done wrong, but I am now very sorry for my poor choices. I believe God has forgiven me and this gives me permission to forgive myself. Now you be quiet and get out of here." Saying those or similar words may seem a bit silly but these words are not that different from what we might say to a domineering outer voice who seeks to tear apart our self-image. Saying words like the above with authority should help us to take control of voices that seek to enslave us and keep us from accepting God's mercy and forgiving ourselves.

- If we continue to have a difficult time forgiving ourselves or accepting God's forgiveness, we may want to seek the help of a good counselor or spiritual guide. Many of us need the help and affirmation of another caring person to help us accept God's mercy and to forgive ourselves. A good friend or skilled guide may help us to see where we are stuck in the forgiveness process and how we can move forward. And they may help us to see that it is okay for us to forgive ourselves of the most heinous act of wrongdoing. If they can forgive us, surely God will forgive us and that should help us to forgive ourselves for not being perfect. We learn from the Scriptures that with Christ there is always mercy awaiting the one who seeks it. If Jesus expects us to forgive another seventy times seven, surely he will do the same for us.

Difficult Questions

The following are some miscellaneous and difficult questions that often come up when the issue of forgiveness is discussed.

Question 1: Why should we forgive someone who has absolutely no remorse for the wrong he or she did?

Needless to say, it is not easy to forgive someone who shows no remorse for what he/she did. If we have to deal with such a person remembering the following may help:

- We forgive another not because our offender deserves our mercy. We forgive them because that is the example our Savior has set for us. He died for us while we were *still* in our sins (see Romans 5:7–8). He forgave his executioners even though they were hardly sorry for the heinous act they had done. We forgive so that the poison of unforgiveness does not continue to hurt us emotionally and spiritually. We must never forget that the choice not to forgive is a choice to allow our offender to continue to hurt us and a choice to give him/her control over us emotionally and spiritually. "The act of forgiveness does not depend on the other taking responsibility for his or her actions. Forgiveness asks only that we take responsibility for ourselves" (Jean Maalouf). When we choose to forgive let us remember who benefits most from our decision to let go—us and not our offender.

- When we choose to forgive an unrepentant offender, we are choosing to take control away from the flow of hatred or animosity that goes on between two people. Lewis Smedes writes, "Waiting for someone to repent before we forgive is to surrender our Future to the person who wronged us." In his book *Forgive and Forget* (Harper & Row, 1984), Smedes quotes an ancient Jewish document called the *Testaments of the Twelve Patriarchs,* which says: "If a man sin against thee...if he repent and confess, forgive him...But if he be shameless, and persisteth in his wrongdoing even so forgive him from the heart, and leave to God the avenging."

Question 2: Aren't there some things that shouldn't be forgiven like terrorist attacks or rape?

It is certainly very normal and human for us to think that some hurts, wrongs, and injustices shouldn't be forgiven. But, if Jesus placed no limit on forgiveness, neither can we. We may all agree that Jesus' executioners should not be forgiven; yet he forgave them. Forgiving helps to take the hatred and revengeful spirit out of the world.

Question 3: What can we do when the hurt or wrong is ongoing? For example, when a spouse or employer continues to be abusive.

It is difficult enough to forgive when the hurt is in the past, but trying to forgive a hurt that is *ongoing* may seem impossible. For this most difficult situation, consider the following suggestions:

- *If possible separate oneself from the situation.* I doubt God expects us to stay with an abusive spouse or employer. While there are situations where such separation is not possible (such as financial reasons), there are times when such separation only demands courage and support from others. In some situations the abused person can almost become emotionally addicted to their abuser and as a result cannot leave him or her. Or the abused person may not be able to imagine a life outside of the present situation. Obviously such a person will need a lot of counseling and support to help him/her separate from a very unhealthy situation. Having said that, a person may, out of Christian conviction, decide to continue loving someone who is very abusive. While such a person may be called stupid by the world and many Christians, in the eyes of God he or she may be a very Christ-like person. It is not for us to judge.

- *If we cannot or choose not to separate ourselves from the abusive environment, we should do our best to confront our abuser.* God does not expect us to be silent doormats in an unjust situation. During his trial we notice how Jesus did speak up to his torturers. We see this especially in his confrontation with Pilate. If we read John's account of Jesus' dialog with Pilate we will immediately see a person who speaks up and is not in any way intimidated by Pilate and his physical power over him (see John 18:28—19:12). In our own time, we have in Mahatma Gandhi and Martin Luther King, Jr., two great examples of people who resisted injustice and yet remained Christian in outlook and practice. (Mahatma Gandhi, though a Hindu by religious profession, respected and practiced the spirit of the Christian gospel more than most Christians.) Sometimes when a wife, for example, learns how to resist the abusive behavior of her husband, her situation improves a great deal.

- *Resist the powers of darkness with prayer.* Where there is abuse and injustice, the devil is very much at work. In Ephesians 6:10–17, Paul reminds us that we are not just fighting flesh and blood but "rulers and authorities." Daily, we are engaged in a spiritual warfare. We need to know the real enemy is the devil at work in the hearts of ungodly people (and also, of course, at work in all of us when we give him a foothold in our lives). I once knew a man who had a very nasty boss. After he had a spiritual conversion he started the practice of "rebuking the evil spirit" that was operating in his boss. Sometimes his prayers brought about very positive results.

- *Try to accept what cannot be changed.* During his public life on earth, Jesus suffered much pain. He suffered mainly because of the truth that he taught and lived. And he promised that his followers would also suffer (see John 16:2–3). When faced with the cross, there are three possible responses. The first is to run away from the cross. In a society that is becoming more pleasure-oriented and self-seeking, there is a great temptation to avoid any kind of pain. The second response is to become so resigned to pain and the evil around us that we do nothing to remove or minimize it. The third option is to do all that we can to diminish or eliminate pain, evil, and suffering and to try patiently to endure what we cannot change, seeing it as part of the cross that Christ has given to us. Such pain and suffering, united to the suffering of Christ, has great power to transform us into the likeness of our crucified Savior.

- *Be gentle with oneself.* Some people in hurting situations are very harsh and judgmental of themselves. Coping with and being Christian in a continuously abusive situation presents an extraordinary challenge. Often in such situations, we think we are sinning because we have hateful and resentful feelings. We need to remember that feelings are neither right nor wrong; they simply exist. Feelings only enter the moral realm when they are expressed in inappropriate ways. When we are in a continuously hurtful situation or have experienced a deep, deep hurt, it is almost impossible not to feel resentful and be bitter. Therefore, we need to remain patient and gentle with our performance and ourselves.

Concluding Remarks

When we have been hurt or unjustly treated by others we have three options:

- We can deny the hurt and injustice and do nothing to free ourselves of it.
- We can become enraged with our offender and *stay* enraged never choosing to work through our hurt and in the process wound ourselves emotionally, spiritually, and physically.
- Or we can opt to cooperate with the grace of God to forgive these hurts—remembering that this option does not exclude bringing our offender to justice if he/she committed some grave injustice against us.

Choosing either of the first two options will be destructive to our emotional, spiritual, and physical health.

Choosing to deal with life's hurts and injustices may be some of the toughest inner work that we will ever engage in, but it will be work that will free us from our emotional prison and free us to live life more joyfully and fully. When we choose to walk and work with our forgiving God, we will become more like him. We will become ambassadors of reconciliation with Christ (see 2 Corinthians 5:17–21). Let us remember to often intercede for all our brothers and sisters who are working at forgiving and reconciling life's hurts.